Book Title:

'Tis the Season for Wintertime Hoof Care: A guide for the horse owner.

THANK YOU FOR YOUR PURCHASE... We hope you enjoy this book.
If this book contains any print errors, contact customer service for a free replacement copy.
We are dedicated to providing you a quality product for an affordable price.

Disclaimer:

Copyright ©2012 Bryan S. Farcus
Revised edition ©2014

ISBN# 978-0-9858241-5-0

Published by:

FARRIER-FRIENDLY™ SERVICES

Athens, OH 45701

Website: www.farrierfriendly.com
Email: farrierfriendly@hotmail.com

A Special Thanks to
. My mother, Bari, for showing me that there is something about the heart of a horse that can nourish the soul. Also, to my wonderful wife, Shannon, for all her hours of proof reading and for always being supportive of my ideas—even the "hair-brain" ones!

Book cover photo: *"Angel in the snow"* by Sarah L. Baker

Table of Contents:

Preface :

Growing up in Northwestern Pennsylvania, the winter season was always something that we, as kids, looked forward to. When the mercury would fall and there was a hint of the first snowflake, our excitement level would rise. It seemed to be a natural, automatic response. As kids, we had no worries about the impending weather; this transition was without thought and it just happened.

When we think about our horses, they also have sort of a "kid-like" response to the winter season. Though, I must admit that I never really gave any thought to how horses coped. It wasn't until my late teens that I began to have even the slightest interest in horses. It was my mother and her side of the family, they were the real *horse people* and it was a true surprise to them when I willingly began to spend time with horses.

I can still recall that first winter—what an eye opener!—helping with those barn chores in the bitter cold weather. One thing that amazed me was how well all the horses handled it; in fact they actually seemed to enjoy it. By the end of that winter, I learned how adaptable our horses can be. As long as we provide them reasonable care by offering enough water, roughage, and a windbreak, they too can enjoy the winter season.

Horses are truly one of the most adaptable creatures known to man and they are certainly one of the best gifts that God has allowed us to share in.

During this season, I would like to extend to each of you all the best, as you begin another year of learning with your horse and I thank you for your interest in *"Farrier-Friendly"*™.

Your friend in horses,

Bryan Farcus MA,CJF-BWFA

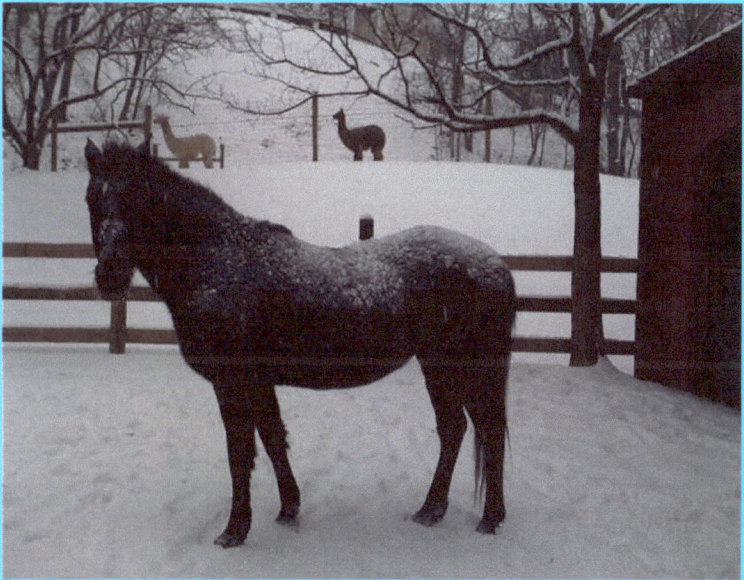

Miss Betty and Buddies

It's that time of year, once again, and I'm finding that the evening chores at the barn are getting a bit hurried. At times, it can be quite a challenge to use-up that last sparkle of daylight. Though I do enjoy the change of seasons, I tend to dread the thought of what inevitably follows. For those of us, who are horse owners, a shift from September to December can be a major concern. Buttoning-up the barn, securing that wobbly fence and getting the winter's hay stored are all time consuming and, perhaps, worrisome tasks. Fortunately, our horses don't have such cumbersome concerns. Horses are one of the most adaptable creatures on earth and with an appropriate level of care; their transition to winter is normally effortless. Seasonal change tends to be gradual, which allows our horses the time to adjust.

Your horse's coat and his hooves are a prime example. Hooves, in particular, are designed to withstand an amazing variety of extremes. For instance, a healthy hoof can accommodate moisture change, tolerate temperature shifts and adjust to various load requirements, all at the same time. To ensure that this process works as nature intended, it's extremely important that all foot structures work in harmony. There are five that are primary. These "functional five" are:

1) The **hoof wall**- designed in a tubular fashion to absorb moisture from the ground, as well as retain its elasticity while weight-bearing.

2) **Sole**- a callus tissue located at the bottom of the foot that functions as a pad to help absorb shock and reduce concussion to the internal bone column.

3) **White Line-** This connective tissue is

approximately 2-4 mm in width and acts as a "buffer [7]

zone" between the wall and the sole. The appearance

of the white line is a major indicator of how healthy

the foot is. It can be referred to as "the window into

the horse's hoof". Any distortion or disturbance in its

connection to the sole is a hint of internal hoof stress.

In such instances, it is a red flag that your farrier

and/or veterinarian need to know about. Simply

committing to routine farrier visits can go a long way

towards treatment and in many cases prevention of

problems.

4) **Frog**- a softer tissue of a triangular shape that

serves to provide traction and aids in the blood

circulation of the limb, due to it expansion

capabilities.

5) **Coronary Band/Periople**- located at the top of

the hoof, where the capsule meets the hair skin of the

leg, is also a major player in the expansion mechanism of the entire hoof. This tissue is analogous to the cuticle of your fingernail. It provides a smooth, flexible connection between the wall and the skin. It also provides us with a great way to monitor the moisture within each hoof. When a hoof is beginning to lose moisture, the periople will become "scaly" or "chalky" in appearance. When over saturation of the hoof occurs the periople will appear "sticky" or "gummy"; quite similar to experiencing "dish-pan hands".

From time-to-time, conscientious horse owners begin to question their horse's ability to brave those cold winter nights. As a practicing farrier, having worked in the "snow belt" regions of northwestern PA and eastern OH, I have witnessed the incredible resilience of horses when faced with those wicked, bone-chilling temperatures. Interestingly, the most questioned condition of frostbite in horses is the least common. Most people assume that the horse's toes chill just as rapidly as their own. Though it is true that horses, like most mammals, protect their vital organs against abnormally low temperatures by shunting blood supply from their extremities to aid in warmth, horses have a remarkable ability to shunt a great deal of blood from their hooves and still maintain normal function of their feet. According to an interview, conducted by Marcia King, Dr. Andris J. Kaneps of the American College of Veterinary Surgeons and professor at Oregon State University stated:

"We don't understand blood shunting of the horse's feet very well, but there is some type of protective role to the feet in cold weather. It's empirical information because we know a horse can stand all day in a snow bank and not get frozen feet, whereas if you or I stood in a snow bank, we'd have frozen feet pretty quickly. The hoof capsule helps protect many of the tissues in the foot and can sustain some level of decreased blood flow, naturally, without being damaged."

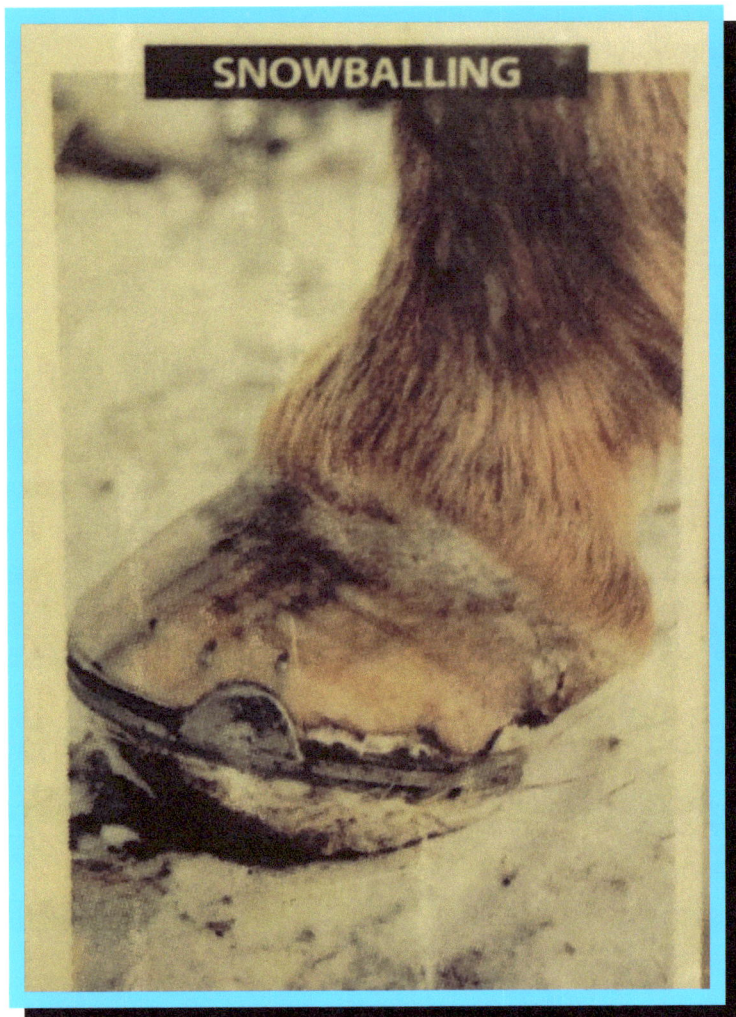

Photo by: Richard Klimesh, CJF

The main reason to shoe your horse for the winter or any time of the year would be to provide comfort. In some pre-existing or chronic type lameness cases, shoeing your horse may be a year-around necessity. In other situations, the type of work/riding you are expecting your horse to do may necessitate shoeing. Providing your horse with enough traction to avoid a slip or fall is important. Jobs, such as, winter trail riding, hunting, or packing will require extra traction for the horse and possible padding on shoes to prevent sole bruising from frozen ground.

✦ *Added benefits, but not without risk ...*

It's extremely important to realize that any wintertime shoeing comes with a little more owner

responsibility and perhaps some risk if proper daily
hoof care is ignored.

A condition that is simply referred to as *snowballing* is the most common cause of horse and, possibly, rider injury, due to the snow compacting inside the bottom of the shod hoof and then freezing to the inner rim of the horseshoe. Snowballing can happen within just a few minutes of your horse traveling on snow, if the consistency of the snow and the temperature is just right.

✦ *Care & Prevention…*

If wintertime shoeing is required, it may be necessary to pick-out your horse's hooves several times per day, depending on the type and amount of snow you encounter. Even horses that are stalled can have an issue with snowballing, with just a few steps out into the snow. In a mild, drier snow conditions, sometimes an oily solution, such as WD-40 or

cooking spray, can be applied to the ground surface of the horseshoe to prevent snow and ice buildup. However, in more extreme snowy conditions it may be necessary to have your farrier add a particular type of *anti-snowball* pad. One most commonly used is a "bubble-type" pad. It will cover the entire bottom of the hoof. This pad is designed with a bubble in the center that allows an in and out action of the bubble with each step the horse takes, helping to prevent snow/ice build-up. Unfortunately, this is still not a fail-proof system. As some horses with tender/flatter soles, may experience more discomfort than benefit. Also, covering a foot with a pad of that nature may, overtime, create common frog bacteria called *Thrush*.

If you think your horse may benefit from wintertime

shoes, I recommend that you contact your farrier well before the snow hits, so that he/she can help you come up with the best possible plan—one that can be both practical for your horse and affordable to you.

And finally, remember... horseshoes must be reset or removed on an average of 6-8wks. to prevent any injury to you or your horse due to overgrown and out of balance feet.

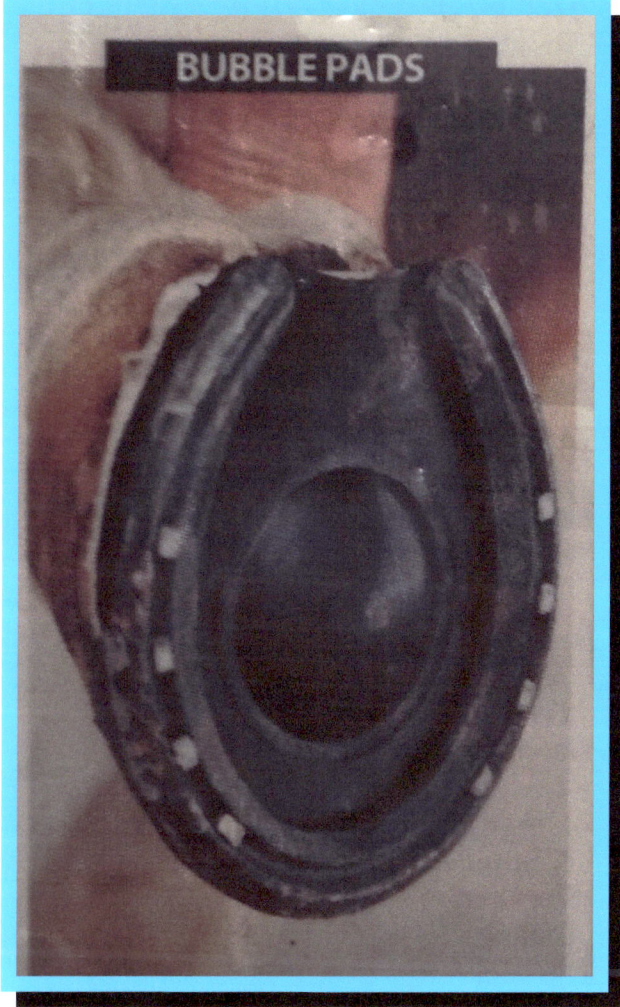

Photo by: Richard Klimesh, CJF

"Ride on & Ride Safe!"

By most accounts, the best advice for preventing any cold weather complication for your horse, is to make sure he has access to enough drinkable water (contrary to popular belief, eating snow is not enough), keep him in an area that allows him to move around freely, offer an adequate amount of forage, and provide a shelter for a chance to get dry and for a windbreak. If he has no access to a shelter, a weatherproof blanket can be beneficial. Many horses are smart about using trees and even each other to stand tail-to-tail as a natural windbreak. Whether your horse is shod or bare footed, it's important to maintain his hoof care. Your farrier can spot subtle changes and take necessary steps to keep your horse's feet in good working order. It's also a good idea to take notice of how your horse postures. Does he seem

stable and sure footed when moving about in the
snow? Is he extremely uncomfortable in his steps
and, perhaps, tender footed? During those wet,
"packing" type snowfalls, a daily hoof picking can be
helpful in preventing ice build-up and snowballing of
the feet. In some cases, frozen mud or other debris
may adhere to the sole and cause bruising. Again,
your hoof pick can help. In both situations, you may
even consider applying a non-stick solution to the
bottom of his hooves. Common household products,
such as Vaseline, cooking spray or WD40 spray can
be very effective. As a general rule, most horses can
tolerate a "dry cold" much easier than a wet or damp
chill. By preparing ahead of time and establishing a
good wintertime routine, before that first flake hits,
you can finally sit back, relax and without any worry
let it snow—After all, *it is the season!*

Glossary of Terms:

Axis BB (Broken-Back): hoof to pastern digit axis line that is visualized to represent a long toe/low heel hoof conformation.

Axis BF (Broken-Forward): hoof to pastern digit axis line that is visualized to represent a short toe/high heel hoof conformation.

Bars: viewed from the bottom of the hoof, minor protrusions present on both sides of the frog, a connective tissue that ties the buttress of the heel to the sole, acts to reinforce the heels.

Bar shoe: general term used to indicate any shoe that is closed or connected at the ends to maximize weight bearing surface, often used to stabilize a weak hoof or support a weakness in a limb.

BBLS: (Basic Body Language System) a term used to identify any system of communicating with the horse through herd instincts, based on predetermined gestures, signals, or cues that are horse logical.

Bulb: located at the back of a hoof connecting the frog and the coronary band, often referred to as the frog band.

Buttress of Heel: the part of the hoof wall that runs to the open end of the foot, often referred to as the point or butt of the heel.

Conformation: an overall view of the horse's entire body, comparing the horse's body structure for symmetry and/or functional alignment.

Commissures: the grooves that are present on either side of the frog, sometimes referenced as the paracuneal sulci.

Corrective shoeing: an approach to shoeing with a major emphasis on changing the horse's stance and/or way of going.

Coronary Band: a band of soft tissue that surrounds the top of each hoof nearest the hairline.

Club footed: a hoof that grows excessively high in the heel as compared to the toe length, there are various degrees of severity, generally considered "clubby" if the horse's hoof-to-pastern is broken-forward, due to a flexor tendon contracture that is extreme enough to distend the coffin joint. this condition may be due to an injury, but most commonly inherited.

Glossary of Terms [continued] :

Deep Digital Cushion: also know as the plantar cushion, a fibro-fatty tissue underlying the frog that functions as a shock absorber.

Degree Pad: wedged shaped pads that are placed between the hoof and the shoe that will raise the hoof and lift the rear surface of a limb.

Deviation: a departure from a predetermined ideal, a term often used in horse conformation analysis to describe crookedness in a limb.

Dynamic Hoof Balance: evaluation of hoof balance as it pertains to the horse in motion, considering how the hoof will land and load.

Frog: a triangular shaped, elastic pad-like tissue that is located at the bottom of the foot that acts to absorb concussion and aid in traction

Gait: a pattern of movement or the way in which the horse travels, certain gaits are natural to all horses but some can be artificial.

Hoof Anatomy: the study of the structure/parts of a hoof.

Hoof Physiology: the study of the function of a hoof.

Glossary of Terms [continued] :

Interfering: a term used to describe the hitting together of a horse's foot to an opposing limb in a manner that restricts the horse's ability to move forward in a comfortable manner.

Keratination: a process whereby the division of horn producing cells accumulate to produce outer layers of hoof wall to protect sensitive tissue, similar to our own nail growth.

LLD (Limb Length Disparity): a condition where the horse suffers from a structural difference of his limbs as a working pair, often a curvature of the spine and/or a clubbed footed conformation is present.

Low-Underrun Heels: When viewed from the side, the heels of the horse are collapsed and low to the ground, the slope or angle of the heel is much lower than that of the toe.

Phalanx -1st : the first bone in the lower limb directly below the fetlock, also known as the long pastern.

Phalanx -2nd: the second bone in the lower limb directly below the fetlock, also known as the short pastern.

Phalanx -3rd: the third and last bone in the lower limb directly below the fetlock, also known as the coffin bone.

Quarter: when viewed from the bottom of the hoof, the region of hoof wall that is between the toe and heel.

Sensitive Laminae: an interlocking, velcro-like tissue within a hoof that is responsible for connecting the hoof wall to the coffin bone.

Seat of corn: viewed from the bottom of the hoof, a junction where the edge of the bar, sole and white-line come together, an area susceptible to attracting debris that can result in a sore spot (corn).

Sole: the flat, ground surface portion of the hoof, responsible for creating a natural pad that is designed to protect the coffin bone.

Static Hoof Balance: a view of hoof balance when the horse is at a stand still, using a geometric reference (X,Y,Z planes) for a three dimensional perspective.

Supportive Shoeing: fitting a shoe with enough length and width to protect and support the entire limb.

Glossary of Terms [continued] :

Therapeutic Shoeing: an approach to shoeing that provides a level of comfort and also attempts to remedy a hoof disease.

Vertical Depth Tolerance: a general reference to the amount of exfoliated sole that is able to be safely trimmed without causing the horse to be tender.

White line: usually yellowish or brown, it is the connective tissue (terminal ends of the sensitive laminea) that bonds the hoof wall to the sole, aids in nail placement.

Helpful Tables & Graphics:

This page is reprinted with permission from the Author of

HORSE FOOT CARE
By Dr. Doug Butler

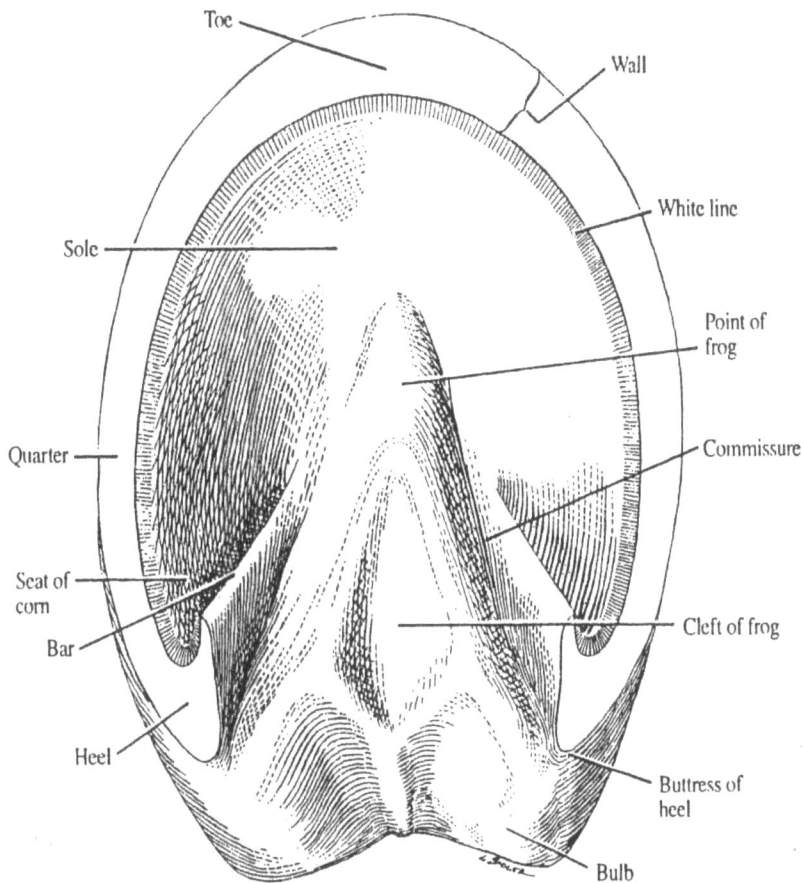

Toe — Wall

White line

Sole —

Point of frog

Quarter —

Commissure

Seat of corn

Bar —

Cleft of frog

Heel

Buttress of heel

Bulb

The parts of the hoof

X

Y

Z

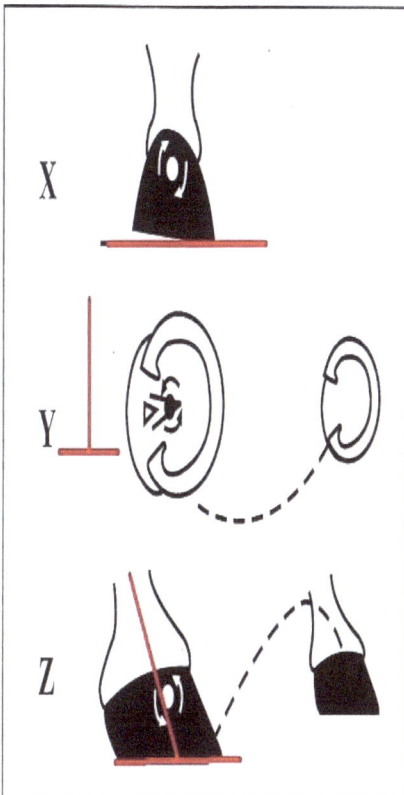

Visualing the 3 dimensions of balance as
applied to Dynamic or Functional balance.

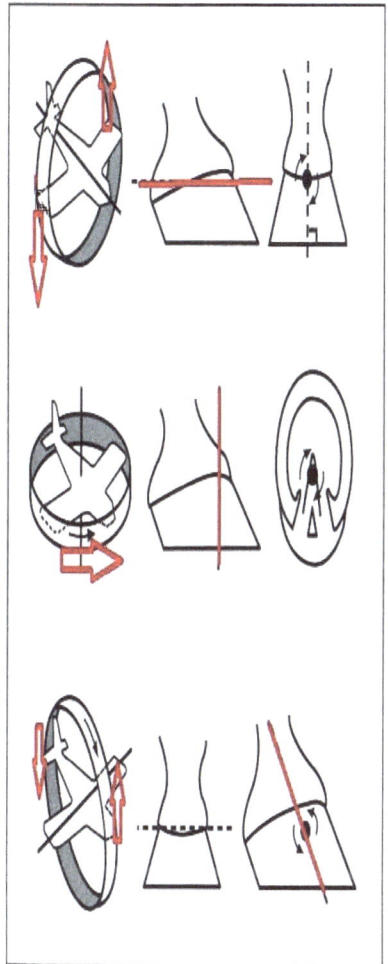

A POSITIVE *"A Healthy Hoof"*	ITS OPPOSITE *"An Unhealthy Hoof"*
Hard/shiny exterior hoof wall.	Soft/cracked, dull exterior wall.
Symmetrically shaped hoof wall.	Asymmetrically shaped hoof wall.
Soft/flexible hair line tissues.	Hard/"crusty" hair line tissues.
Soft/flexible frog tissues.	Hard or diseased frog tissues.
Parallel growth pattern of toe and heel lengths.	Reversed growth pattern of toe and heel lengths.
Normal cupping of the sole. (bottom surface of hoof is arched allowing for edge of hoof wall to contact ground first)	Extremely flat or "dropped" sole. (bottom surface of hoof is contacting the ground before edge of hoof wall)
Hoof wall thickness approx. 2 x greater than "white line" thickness.	Hoof wall thickness less than the "white line" thickness (white line distortion)
"White line" region and sole surface adjoin without deep cracks present.	Deep cracks existing between the "white line" region and the sole surface.

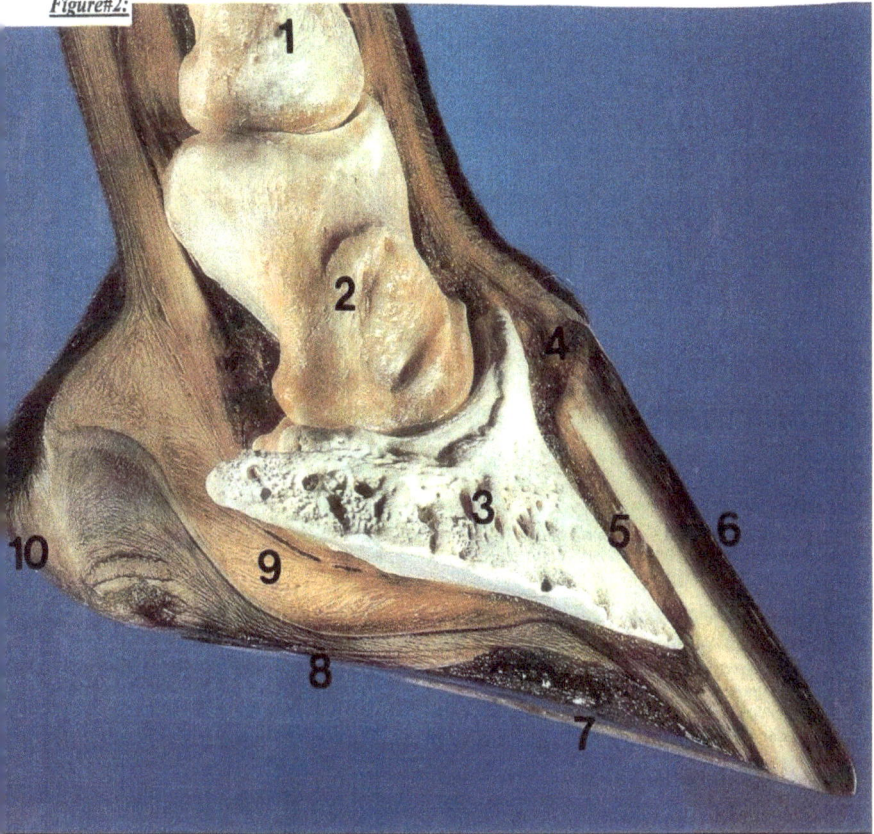

Figure#2:

LATERAL OBLIQUE VIEW OF EQUINE DIGIT. Soft tissue is removed from one side of the phalanges.

1. First Phalanx (long pastern).
2. Second Phalanx (short pastern).
3. Third Phalanx (coffin bone).
4. Coronary Band.
5. Sensitive Laminae.
6. Hoof wall (toe region).
7. Sole.
8. Frog.
9. Deep Digital Cushion.
10. Bulb of foot.

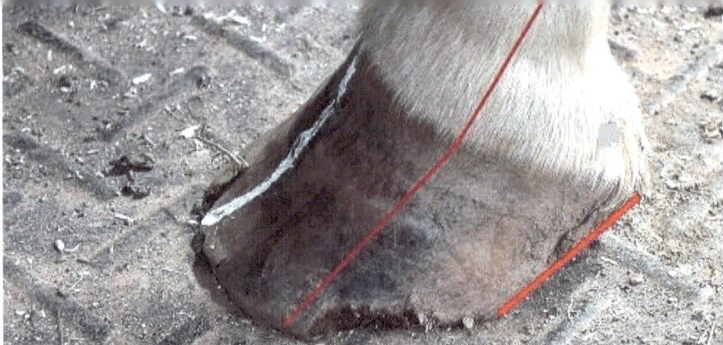

Broken-Back Axis

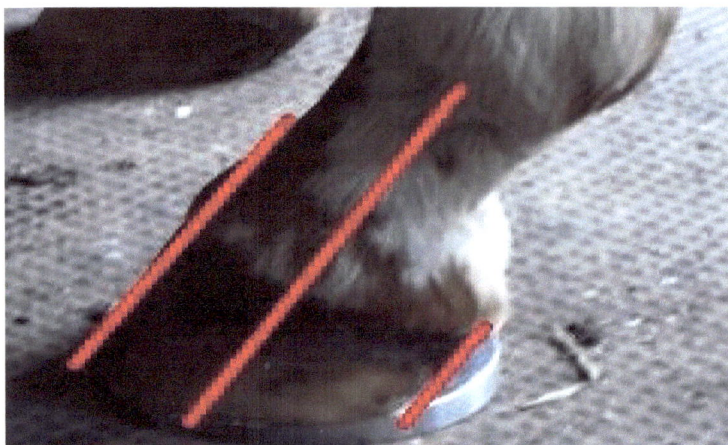

Balanced

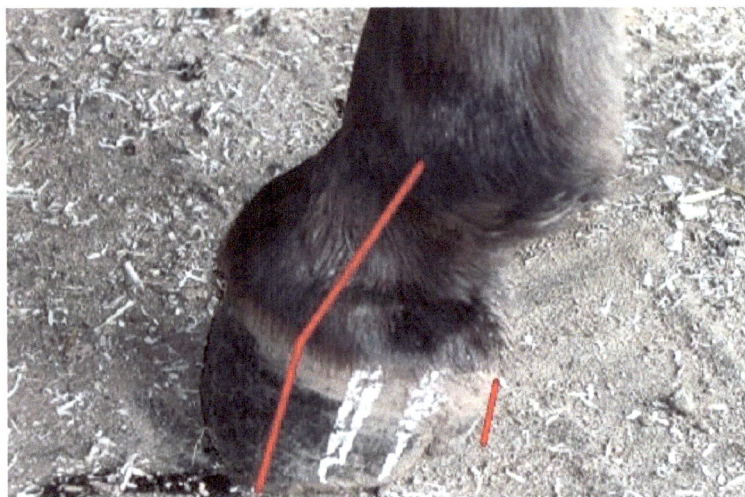

Broken-Forward Axis

Photos by: Bryan Farcus CJF

Noticing Limb Length Disparity (*LLD*)...

BELOW: a view of a balanced and symmetrical top-line.

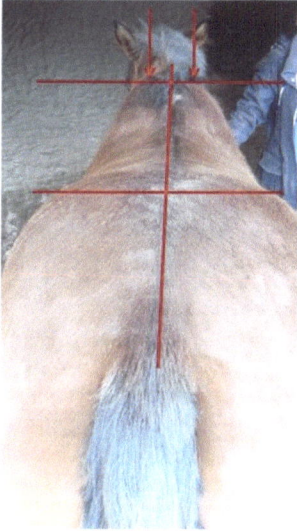

Photo by: Bryan S. Farcus   Learning to view your horse's top-line can offer you a better understanding of why the feet are as they are. Using a top-down approach to assess hoof balance can help a farrier make better trimming and shoeing decisions.

NEXT PAGE (Below): a view of a typical dropped shoulder/ but this horse is functionally sound ,as long as he is trimmed and shod to support and promote a more balanced top-line, as opposed to corrective shoeing for the hooves only.

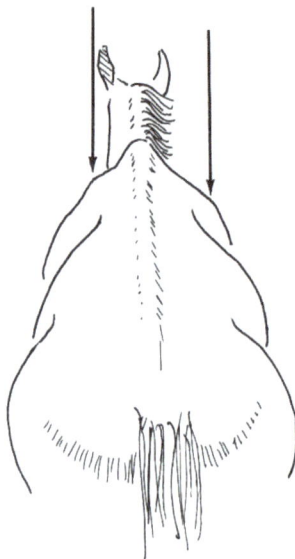

Diagram courtesy of King Lamadora

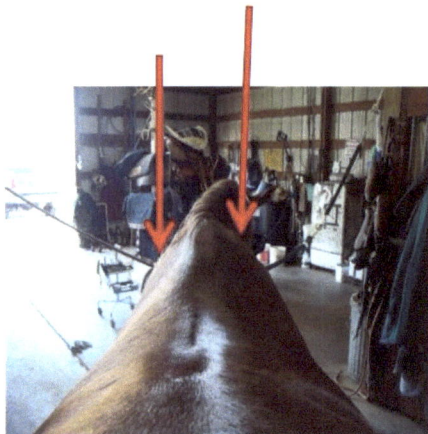

Photo courtesy of Kirk Underschultz CJF

Above:same horse : **Before** trimming/shoeing
Below:same horse :After

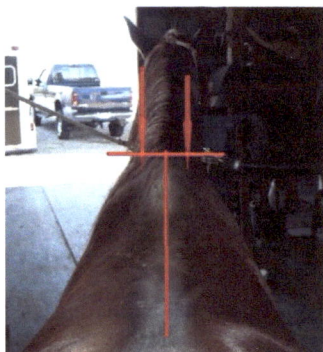

Top-line imbalances can result due to a variety of conformational issues. Of the most common are: *Club footedness, Low-underrun heels, Curvature of the spine, Dropped shoulder/or hip, Congenital bone length differences within limbs.* Some are functional deviations while others are not.

Resources & Recommending Reading :

RESOURCES...

American Farrier's Journal , Lessiter Publications

PBM : A Diary of Lameness, Anthony Gonzales

The Principles of Horseshoeing (P3),Doug &Jacob Butler

Maximum Hoof Power, Richard Klimesh

WEBSITES...

www.horseshoes.com
www.petplace.com
www.thehorse.com
www.horsekeeping.com/horse-articles

ASSOCATIONS...

AAPF, American Association of Professional Farriers, www.professionalfarriers.com

AFA, American Farrier's Association, www.americanfarriers.org

BWFA, Brotherhood of Working Farriers, www.bwfa.net

About The Author :

Bryan S. Farcus MA, CJF-BWFA ~

For the past 25 years, Bryan has been combining the skills of horseshoeing, teaching, and riding. He is a Certified Journeyman Farrier through the Brotherhood of Working Farriers Association (BWFA) and also holds a certification in Equine Massage Therapy. Bryan's other accomplishments include both a Master of Arts degree with a specialization in equine education and a Bachelor of Science degree in the area of business.

For more than ten years, Bryan was the director/ instructor of a Farrier Studies program at an international equestrian college and a guest instructor for others, as well.

These days, he continues his teaching by offering various "horsemanship for horseshoeing" programs. Upon invitation, Bryan presents demonstrations and group discussions on basic hoof care and horsemanship, in order to promote the advancement of equine education. Bryan is also the creator of a select line of "*Farrier-Friendly*™" products and currently authors a series of "*Farrier-Friendly*™" articles that appear in horse magazines throughout the US. Bryan currently works with horses and their owners in Ohio and West Virginia. You can visit him at:

www.farrierfriendly.com or e-mail: farrierfriendly@hotmail.com

.

www.ingramcontent.com/pod-product-compliance
Lightning Source LLC
Chambersburg PA
CBHW041755050426
42443CB00023B/12